The *GOLF Magazine*
Putting Handbook

Other titles in the series

The *GOLF Magazine* Golf Fitness Handbook
The *GOLF Magazine* Mental Golf Handbook
The *GOLF Magazine* Course Management Handbook
The *GOLF Magazine* Full Swing Handbook
The *GOLF Magazine* Short Game Handbook

The *GOLF Magazine*
Putting Handbook

Peter Morrice
and the Editors of *GOLF Magazine*

Photography by Sam Greenwood

The Lyons Press

First Lyons Press edition, 2000

Printed in the United States of America
Design and composition by Compset, Inc.

10 9 8 7 6 5 4 3 2 1

The Library of Congress Cataloging-in-Publication Data

Morrice, Peter.
    The Golf magazine putting handbook/Peter Morrice
the editors of Golf magazine.
        p. cm.
    ISBN: 1–55821–939–0
    1. Putting (Golf)—Handbooks, manuals, etc.
I. Title: Putting handbook. II. Golf magazine (New
York, N.Y.: 1991) III. Title.

GV979.P8 M67 2000
796.352'35—dc21
                                                    00-023815

Acknowledgments

Many people contributed to the making of this book. First, my gratitude to George Peper, editor-in-chief of *GOLF Magazine*, who trusted this project in my hands. I am also indebted to Jonathan Abrahams for his contributions to the manuscript. And to Bryan Oettel and Jill Hindle at The Lyons Press, whose editorial skills and professionalism made them perfect partners. For the photographs, I thank *GOLF Magazine* staff photographer Sam Greenwood, as well as Mike Stubblefield, Dennis Blake, Mike LaBrutto, and Wendy Obenrader, who modeled for and helped with the photo shoots. Lastly, a big thanks to my family and friends for their patience and constant encouragement during late nights and long weekends. Special recognition goes to my parents: my father for the golf, my mother for the writing.

Contents

8   CONTENTS

Foreword

At *GOLF Magazine* we use two methods to determine the content to include each month: surveys and guts. In the survey method, questionnaires are sent to thousands of our subscribers, asking what topics they enjoy most, which kinds of articles they prefer, etc. In the guts method, we editors simply use our intuition as kindred, hopelessly addicted golfers.

But no matter which method we use, the number-one answer is always the same: instruction. "Give us more instruction," has been the mandate from our readers ever since the magazine began publishing, forty years ago. The reason is simple: A golfer is happiest when his game is improving.

Recently, however, we've learned a couple of things about how to present our instruction. Number one, you like it short and sweet. After all, most of the current populace was raised on television, sound bites, and quick delivery of information, from beepers to e-mail. More than ever, we like our messages short and to the point.

And the "to the point" part is just as important as the "short" part. For the last decade or so, the most popular portion of *GOLF Magazine* has been the buff-colored section called "Private Lessons," which brings together custom-tailored instruction for five different kinds of golfers: low handicappers, high handicappers, short but straight hitters, long but crooked hitters, and senior golfers. In this way, we're able to speak more personally to our readers and help them more individually with their games.

Why am I telling you all this? Because the same kind of thinking went into the book that is now in your hands. When the people at The Lyons Press came to talk to us about a partnership in golf book publishing, we gave them our mantra for success: instruction, succinct and focused. The result is the *GOLF Magazine* series of guides, each written concisely, edited mercilessly, and dedicated entirely to one key aspect of playing the game.

Each *GOLF Magazine* guide assembles a wealth of great advice in a package small enough to carry in your golf bag. We hope you'll use these pages to raise your game to a whole new level.

George Peper
Editor-in-Chief
GOLF Magazine

The *GOLF Magazine*
Putting Handbook

Introduction

Admit it: You hate putting. Before you object, there's plenty of evidence to support this contention. Consider: If you shoot ninety for eighteen holes with 36 putts (an average of two per green), 40 percent of your strokes are made with the putter. Compare that to maybe 20 strokes with the wedge, 14 with the driver, and another 20 or so with all the remaining clubs in the bag. But you don't spend 40 percent of your practice time putting. Nobody does, because *everybody* hates putting.

If people really liked to putt, there'd be multi-tiered practice putting facilities popping up all over the country. Holes would be reserved by the hour, and people would rush from work to roll a few before dinner. And the average American handicap would be way down. Fact is, putting has the biggest effect on how well you score, yet folks would much rather spend time whacking balls off rubber mats with the driver, a club that's used less than half as much.

Then again, maybe you don't hate putting; maybe you just don't understand it. It can be something to enjoy, obsess about even, if you approach it not just as a shorter version of all the other shots you hit in golf, but a completely different game in itself. It's contained and precise; a thinking man's game, like billiards or chess. It doesn't require near the amount of coordination it takes to crush a 270-yard drive, yet it would be hard to find a physically more awkward feeling than missing a three-foot putt. It's mysterious and paradoxical: The great Ben Hogan, perhaps the finest and most consistent ball-striker ever, once said, "I'd enjoy the game a lot more if I didn't have to putt." Hogan won nine major titles, including back-to-back U.S. Opens in 1950 and 1951, but nobody ever accused him of being particularly strong on the greens. Perhaps he didn't understand putting either.

But don't let that fool you into thinking that good putting is some sort of mystical blessing bestowed by the golf gods. Success with the putter comes from a simple formula: a combination of proper technique and a confidence that comes from knowing what you're doing as you stand over each putt. And anybody can make that happen. The technique is not particularly complicated or physically demanding, and you don't have to be a rocket scientist to read greens and understand smart putting strategy. So, there's no reason why a high handicapper can't be a good putter and a middle-handicapper a great putter well before either masters the game from tee to green.

If that doesn't inspire you, go back to that hypothetical 90 you shot with the 36 putts. Say you eliminate a few three putts and sink a couple of 10-footers that you ordinarily miss. Now you've taken 30 putts, and that bloated 90 is suddenly a lean and mean 84, a much more exciting number to see at the bottom of the scorecard. The next round you play, there's less pressure on your game from tee to green because *you know* you're putting well. You relax, swing a little freer, and *presto*—hit four more greens in regulation than you did the round before. Add your 30 putts, and you're actually threatening to break 80! A 10-stroke improvement, and that's without hitting one driver off a rubber mat.

Of course, 10 strokes is optimistic. It's completely plausible for a high handicapper, but maybe there's only six or seven strokes to be had for a 15-handicapper. And maybe a single-digit player can only hope to cut three or four—but those are still precious strokes. Nevertheless, one thing is certain: Whatever your level of play, the fastest way to take it to the next level is by improving your play on the greens. You may have hated putting before, but you'll love it when your scores start to drop.

If this reads like a sermon on the value of putting, fine—the purpose of this book is not only to teach, but to inspire as well. You'll have the opportunity to familiarize (or refamiliarize) yourself with the fundamentals, brush up on strategy, and learn some new ways to make those sessions on the practice green actually bearable. You'll also find some of the most helpful putting tips ever published in *GOLF Magazine,* in a feature called "Best Tip." Not that any of it will ever make putting as exciting as nailing a perfect drive or sticking an approach shot close to the pin, but it should show you that real improvement is well within your reach. And that's the exciting part.

The Setup

Any discussion of putting technique has to begin with two acknowledgments. The first one is that at the end of the day, there is no "right" way to putt. Because putting is such a make-or-break part of the game, whatever happens to get the ball in the hole in the least number of strokes is perfect. If you digest all the information in this book and then realize that you're deadly from inside 10 feet standing on one foot, stick with it. That technique is right for you. On the Tour, making putts is the difference between big money and just scraping by. So it's not surprising to see a wide variety of putting styles among the pros, from tall posture to crouched posture, from narrow to wide stances, from short, poppy strokes to long, slow sweeps. Players do what works.

Second acknowledgment: Even though there are no hard-and-fast rules of putting technique, there are a handful of fundamentals that work for most golfers. Those fundamentals will be the primary focus of the technical section of this book. More specifically, most golfers will find the greatest success by making a putting stroke that is controlled almost entirely by moving the arms and shoulders as a unit, while the hands simply follow along. *For most golfers,* it's easier to keep the putterface pointed at the target if the hands and wrists aren't doing anything except stabilizing the club.

For sure, there have been great putters who used wristy strokes—and "alternative techniques" will also be addressed in the book—but most of the fundamentals of grip, stance, and alignment are designed to promote an arms-and-shoulders stroke, because that's the simplest way to do it. And simple means easy to do well, and easy to repeat. So, before you jump to the conclusion that your stroke is decidedly idiosyncratic, get to know and understand these basic fundamentals. See how they work for you. If you're a better player, use them to check yourself. A prolonged stretch of inconsistency might indicate that you've wandered too far away from them. But no matter your level of play, let simplicity be the foundation of your putting stroke. Once that's established, you can go about discovering the nuances that will make your stroke distinctly yours.

The Pendulum Motion

Imagine a tower with a pendulum hanging from a fixed point at the top, like a grandfather clock. The pendulum swings back and forth while the clock tower remains still. It's a time-worn yet perfect analogy for an arms-and-shoulders putting stroke. Your body is the tower, and your shoulders, arms, hands, and putter form the pendulum. The fixed point is right between your shoulders—the very top of your sternum. The body remains still while the shoulders, arms, hands, and club swing back and through. If you think in those terms, it's easy to see why grip and stance are such important parts of putting. If your hands and wrists move independently, the pendulum breaks down. If your stance is unstable, the pendulum won't swing from a fixed point.

You can see and feel the pendulum motion by standing in front of a full-length mirror without a golf club. Bend forward from the hips and clap your palms together so your hands, arms, and shoulders form a large triangle (remember this triangle image, as we'll come back to it often). Keeping the palms together, swing the arms back and through by rocking the shoulders. Notice how the triangle is maintained throughout the motion; the relationship between the hands, arms, and shoulders never changes. This is the

To feel the pendulum, swing your hands and arms back as a triangle.

essence of the arms-and-shoulders stroke; it changes slightly when there's an actual club in your hands, but your grip and stance should be designed to make the difference as small as possible.

As you swing through, maintain the shape of the triangle.

Grip

When the palms face each other directly below your sternum, as they do when you create the triangle, they are perpendicular to the target line. In other words, the back of the left hand and the palm of the right hand face the hole, which makes it easier to swing the arms back and through on a straight line. That's the goal with the putting grip; there are many different variations, but you'll find it easiest to make a straight arms-and-shoulders stroke if the palms face each other.

Fortunately, most putter grips are designed to help you do this. Find the flat ridge running down the middle of the grip; if you hold the club with both thumbs resting on top of that ridge, your palms will be effectively facing each other. (The palms don't *really* face each other, not as they do in the triangle exercise, because the right hand is below the left on the grip.) Generally, the hands are closer together on the putter than they are in a regular full-swing grip. That way, they operate much more as a single unit, keeping the connection between the arms and putter as seamless as possible so the pendulum can swing without any unnecessary complications.

In the traditional Vardon, or overlapping, grip used in the full swing, the club sits in the fingers of

The grip should run down the middle of the left palm.

the left hand, allowing the wrist the necessary mobility to hinge during the swing. With a putter, however, the grip is nestled into the palm of the hand, locked right into the channel created by the thumb pad and the heel. Holding the handle in the palm not only points the back of the hand to the target, but has the effect of immobilizing the left wrist as well, so the swinging of the putter can be a natural extension of the arms-and-shoulders movement. (Incidentally, this is why some players prefer a thicker grip on their putters—it makes it easier to grip in the palm, thereby reducing the risk of unwanted contribution from the hands and wrists.) The left thumb sits on top of the grip, on the flat ridge, and, although the fingers should never apply more than moderate pressure to the handle, the bulk of the squeezing in the left hand is done by the last two fingers.

Place the right hand on the grip so the right thumb pad covers the left thumb and the right thumb rests on the flat ridge. Wrap all four fingers of the right hand around the handle so the palm directly faces the target. In the reverse-overlap grip— the accepted "standard" for putting—the left forefinger, and sometimes the middle finger, too, rests on top of the fingers of the right hand. It's this overlapping of fingers that makes it possible for the hands to be as close together as possible. First try overlapping the left forefinger only. Does the grip feel as if it's seated securely in your left palm between the heel and thumb pad? If it doesn't, you

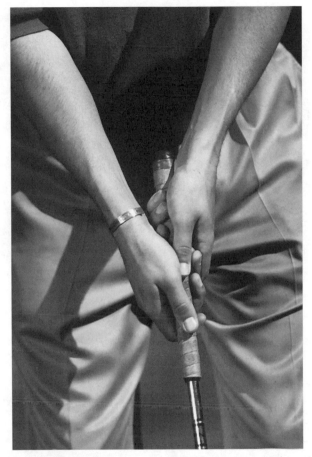

Both thumbs should sit on the flat ridge on top of the grip.

can try extending the left forefinger so it points down the shaft, across the first knuckles of the fingers of the right hand. Let the middle finger of the left hand overlap the pinkie or ring finger of the

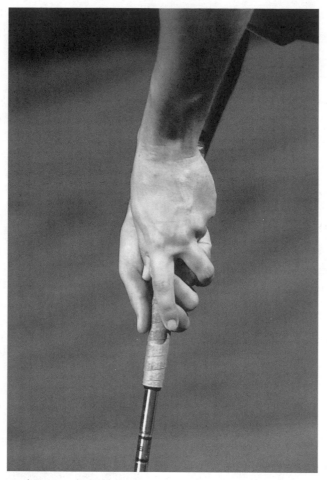

In the popular reverse-overlap grip, the left forefinger "overlaps" the right hand.

right. You may find it easier to set the grip in the palm of the left hand this way. Certainly with two fingers overlapping, the hands are closer together. If you feel like you can control the putter with this grip, it's a great way to keep the hands operating as a single unit.

Already you can see that there are viable options when it comes to gripping the putter. If you decide to experiment, remember the goals of a conventional grip: to keep the hands close together, the palms facing each other, and wrist action to a minimum. With a good grip, you have in place the critical first piece of the putting puzzle.

Stance and Posture

Like the hands, the position of the body has a major effect on your ability to make a straight, smooth pendu-

First and Foremost

The reverse-overlap grip was invented by Walter J. Travis, a putting pioneer who won three of the first four U.S. Amateur Championships of the 20th century. A late bloomer who didn't take up the game until his mid-30s, Travis was a notoriously short hitter who compensated by infuriating his opponents with stellar putting. Nobody complained about his grip (he later taught it to the great Bobby Jones), but his putter—one of the first center-shafted models, known as "The Schenectady"—was banned in Britain after he won the 1904 British Amateur.

lum stroke. Go back to the triangle exercise: If you stand perfectly straight and tall, there won't be any room for your arms to swing back and through; your body will be in the way. Similarly, if your stance points 45 degrees to the left, your arms will want to swing that way, instead of to the target. Positioning the body to putt is not a complicated process, but it is something to be meticulous about. Good body position breeds a good stroke; poor position breeds compensations and mistakes.

In a standard putting stroke, only the pendulum moves—the shoulders, arms, and hands. The rest of the body—legs, hips, torso, head—remains still from the moment the stroke starts until after contact is made. You should always be relaxed, but at the same time, your stance serves to lock your body into place.

Start without a club. Stand with your feet 15 to 20 inches apart and square to the target line (imagine a line drawn across the tops of your toes; if that line is parallel to the line running from the ball to the target, your stance is square). Stability is the prime objective here, so distribute your weight evenly between each foot and allow the knees to flex slightly. Locking the knees may feel stable, but it actually creates tension in the body, which will eventually creep into your stroke. Bend forward slightly from the hips; notice how this allows the arms to hang from the shoulders, away from the torso. If you feel your weight moving onto your toes, you're bending too far.

This posture puts the body in position to make a straight-back, straight-through pendulum stroke. It's a square setup—if you drew imaginary lines across the feet, knees, hips, and shoulders, all would be parallel to the target line. Also, notice

With proper posture, the hands hang below the shoulders.

from a down-the-line view how the hands hang under the shoulders. That way, they can easily swing straight back and through on a line parallel to the target line.

Now try it with a putter and a ball. Everything stays the same: feet square, knees slightly flexed, torso bent forward from the hips, hands directly under shoulders . . . plus one more thing. Draw an-

A square stance promotes an on-line stroke.

other imaginary line—this time from your eyes to the ball. That line should be vertical, or very close to vertical, indicating that your eyes are over the ball. This is a must if you're going to see the line of the putt clearly. Otherwise, you're looking at the line from an odd angle, which will distort your perception. Generally, if your eyes are well inside the ball, what appears to be a straight line at the hole will actually point to the right of the hole; if the eyes are outside the ball, what appears to be a straight line will actually point to the left. Only if your eyes are over the ball can you be sure that what you see is what you actually get.

BEST TIP: Stay Balanced

Here are two quick ways to make sure that your body is balanced at the setup, with the arms hanging naturally from the shoulders: 1. If you lift the putter off the ground slightly, it should remain in place, not drift one way or another; 2. Have a friend try to push you off balance. If you're set up properly, it shouldn't have much effect. If you stumble, you weren't very stable in your setup.

—Gregor Jamieson, *GOLF Magazine*
Top 100 Teacher

BEST TIP: Check Your Eyeline

You can be sure that your eyes are over the ball by dropping a second ball from the bridge of your nose; it should hit the ball you're addressing. But it's just as important that your eyeline be parallel to the target line. To check this, take your stance, then hold your putter horizontally at waist level so it is directly under your eyes. If your eyes are over the ball, the shaft should appear to cover the ball; and you know your eyeline is parallel to the target line when you swivel your head and see that the shaft points directly at the hole.

—Eddie Merrins, *GOLF Magazine*
Top 100 Teacher

Square vs. Open

It's simplest to putt with your feet—and the rest of your body—perfectly parallel to the target line, but it's not uncommon to see good players adopting an open stance, in which an imaginary line drawn across the feet angles to the left of the target. Two of the best putters in history, Jack Nicklaus and Ben Crenshaw, have frequently used an open stance, claiming that it makes it easier to see the line of the putt. While that may be true, understand that if your feet are angled to the left of the target, your shoulders probably will be, as well. This alignment will then encourage your arms to swing in the same direction—to the left. Given that, the only way to

Arnie's Unusual Stance

How important is it for your body to be stable? If you go by the great Arnold Palmer, at his best one of the top pressure putters ever, a still body is crucial, no matter what the cost. Palmer was an athletic, charismatic player when his aggressive style of play captured the world's imagination in the 1950s and '60s, but he looked rather unconventional doing it. His full swing was a fast, swiping motion, and his putting stance looked as if he was a long way from a bathroom—and knew it. Knees knocked, feet pigeon-toed, thighs pinched together, he bent way over from the hips to get close to the ball. It wasn't pretty, but it served to lock his body into place so the only thing moving during the stroke would be his shoulders, arms, and hands. And the results he achieved speak for themselves.

swing the putterhead straight down the target line is to reroute it with the hands and arms during the stroke, which is probably more complication than you want to add to your putting motion.

Nicklaus and Crenshaw pulled it off because both had razor-sharp touch in their prime, but for the average golfer, it's much more practical to adopt a square stance. With a square setup, the arms can just follow the lead of the shoulders, without any extra manipulation required.

To Crouch or Not to Crouch

How much should you crouch over when you putt? Again, look at Nicklaus and Crenshaw: Jack always crouched as much as anybody on Tour, while Ben stood tall. Both, obviously, can be fantastic ways to putt. But keep this in mind: Crouching gets you closer to the ball, which can offer a better sense of control, but it also creates angles in the elbows and wrists. For some, those angles can destabilize the triangle formed by the shoulders, arms, and hands, so the shoulders are no longer in complete control of the stroke.

Standing tall, on the other hand, allows the arms to hang straight, or nearly straight, from the shoul-

Crouching over can bolster feel but complicate the stroke.

ders. Being farther from the ball doesn't provide the same sense of control, but you may find it easier to make a smooth pendulum stroke if the arms and wrists are essentially straight and the integrity of the triangle is maintained. Experiment to find what feels best for you.

Standing tall can simplify the stroke but may reduce feel.

The Importance of Ball Position

All theories aside, the putting stroke is not a perfect pendulum motion. In order for that to happen, the putter would have to be built like a croquet mallet, so the arms and shaft could form a vertical line down from the shoulders to the ball. And the shoulders would have to make a perfectly vertical rocking motion, like a hanger on a coat rack.

In reality, the putter is more like a hockey stick, with the shaft angled toward the player. Also, the shoulders don't rock on a perfectly vertical line; they rotate around the spine, as they do in the full swing. As a result, the motion that the putterhead makes during the stroke is *pendulum-like*, but also slightly rounded. That is, not only does the putterhead lift off the ground as it swings back, it also moves slightly to the inside of the target line. As it swings through, it returns down to the target line, then swings up and through to the inside again. It's not very pronounced, and in most cases, it's not even noticeable, but that rounded path is precisely why ball position is critical.

Consider how this path affects the angle of the putterface. When the putterhead goes back slightly inside the line, the putterface naturally rotates open relative to the target. It returns to square at the bottom of the swing arc, stays square for a couple of inches, then rotates closed to the target as the putterhead swings through. So, all else being equal, unless you make contact when the putterhead is within a couple of inches of the bottom of the swing arc, the ball will not roll on the line you've intended. And that's not all. In order for the ball to roll as smoothly as possible, contact must be made when the putterhead is moving parallel to the ground or just slightly on the upswing. If contact is made too early or too late, the ball may skid excessively or hop before rolling, both of which can affect distance control. In other words, you can make a perfect stroke and still miss—and miss badly—if you haven't positioned the ball in your stance correctly.

The good news is that the legs and torso don't move during the stroke, so the low point of the swing arc will generally be in the same place relative to your body every time. To find that spot, go back to the pendulum; the low point of a pendulum's arc is opposite the fixed point where the top of the pendulum connects to the tower. Now think in terms of the triangle exercise: The fixed point is a spot between your shoulders, at the top of the sternum. When the hands are directly under that spot, they are at the bottom of the swing arc. That should be your reference point when positioning your body to the ball.

The putterface should make contact at the low point or just slightly ahead of it (remember, you've got a two-inch window before the putterface begins to rotate off-line). So, position the ball just ahead of the middle of your sternum, about an inch. Assuming your weight is evenly distributed between both feet, that's far enough forward to ensure you don't hit the ball with a descending blow, which can

For optimum contact, play the ball one inch ahead of your sternum.

pinch the ball against the turf and influence the roll. It's also far enough back in your stance that the putterface will still be square to the target, assuming your stroke hasn't broken down.

You might wonder why the sternum is used as the initial point of reference for ball position, and not the feet. That would be simpler, wouldn't it, considering that they're so much closer to the ball? Yes, but the feet aren't always reliable. Consider this: If you position the ball just ahead of center relative to your feet, it will also be just ahead of the center of your sternum—if your weight is evenly distributed between both feet. But if you favor the front leg in your stance (Greg Norman and Nick Faldo do it), your torso shifts forward with your weight, so that same ball position—just ahead of center in your stance—will actually be *behind* the center of your sternum. You'll make contact before the putterhead reaches the bottom of its arc and trap the ball against the green. On the other hand, if you use your sternum as the reference point, you can be sure the ball position is correct every time.

A Word on Aim

All these specifics about the setup are actually only half of what you need to hit the ball the way you want. Aim is the other factor. Good aim is about setting the putterface square to the target; a good setup aligns the body relative to the putterface. Since aim is closely associated with the routine of actually executing a putt on the course, it will be discussed in the next chapter, "The Stroke."

The Stroke

Why does putting have to be so complicated? It's just a short little stroke made with a short little club. It's easy—certainly easier than hitting a full shot with, say, a 3-iron. Right?

Well, kind of. It's easier to make solid contact on a putt than it is on a long-iron shot, but in other ways, a putt is much more demanding. First of all, there's far less margin for error. If you hit a 3-iron from 190 yards to a green that's 20 yards wide, you can have varying degrees of success. Hitting the ball next to the pin is great, but just getting it on the green is pretty good, too. For that matter, missing the green but leaving yourself an easy chip shot isn't so bad, either—you still have a good chance at par. You can miss your target by 10 yards—that's 30 feet—and still feel good about yourself.

With putting, the target is only 4¼ inches wide, and there's only one way to be successful: by making the ball go in the hole. Missing is failure, whether it's by an inch or a foot, unless you're a long way from the hole and just trying to get down in two. But from inside 15 feet, there are only misses—which are no fun—and bad misses, when you leave yourself in position where you might miss again.

And what about distance control? You know approximately how far that 3-iron is going to go if you hit it well. So you only use it when you're the appropriate distance from the green; if you're closer, you take less club and make virtually the same swing. Distance control, for the most part, is out of your hands: The loft of the club and length of the shaft largely determine how far the ball will go. But on the green, the putter is the only club you use, regardless of distance. You determine how far the ball will roll based on how much effort you put into the stroke; it's all on you. So it may not be a physically challenging move, but the putting stroke demands a better sense for direction and distance than any other shot in golf.

A more familiar way to describe direction and distance on the green is by using the words "line" and "speed." To make an effective stroke for any given putt, you need to know what the line of the putt is (the path the ball will take to the hole) and have a sense for the speed (how hard to hit the ball so that it reaches the hole). These factors are fairly simple on a short, straight putt, but if the green is sloped between the ball and the hole, they're dependent on each other: You can't know the right line of a putt unless you have a feel for the speed; and the proper speed varies based on what line you want the ball to take. In that case, understanding line and speed is a process in itself, something that will be explored at length in Chapter Three. First, you have to be able to hit the ball straight. And that begins with proper alignment.

Aim and Alignment

Think in terms of a straight, 10-foot putt. As with full shots, it's easiest to aim the putterface to the hole first, then align your body perpendicular to the putterface. To begin the process, the putterface should be square—at a right angle to the line of the putt. Most putters have a little horizontal line etched into the top of the head designed to help you make sure the face is square. Once the face is square, align your body accordingly, starting with your feet. In a square setup, the lines of your feet,

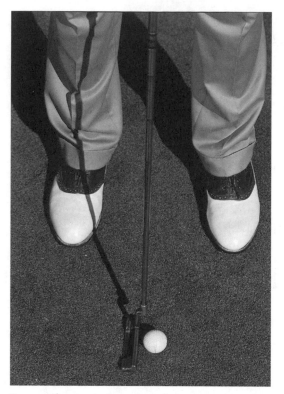

Square the putterface first, then set your stance perpendicular to the face.

knees, hips, and shoulders are parallel to the line of the putt, or perpendicular to the putterface. So, with square aim and alignment and a straight-back, straight-through stroke that returns the putterface to the same square position at impact, the ball will roll perfectly straight.

Aligning yourself for putts that break (curve to the right or left because of undulations in the green) is only slightly different. Instead of aiming the putterface at the hole, square it to the line on which the ball should start. That is, if the putt breaks six inches from right to left, aim the putterface six inches right of the hole, then align your body square to the putterface. From there, make the same straight-back, straight-through stroke you would for a straight putt. It's really that simple.

Spot Putting

Aiming the putterface is easy when the hole is three feet away, but what if it's 20 feet? It's much tougher to be precise and, therefore, feel confident that you're aiming the putter and yourself in the right direction. Wouldn't it be a shame to make a perfect stroke and miss the putt because your putterface and body were aligned just a fraction off-line?

Try spot putting instead. Crouch behind the ball and picture in your mind the line it will take to the hole. Then, choose a spot—an old ball mark or discolored patch of grass—about three feet in front of the ball and on that imaginary line. Instead of aim-

For accurate aim, line up to a spot a few feet in front of the ball.

ing the putterface at the hole, aim it to the spot you've chosen, three feet away. It's much easier to be sure of yourself with such a close target. Then, align your body perpendicular to the putterface and make your stroke. If you've read the putt correctly, the ball will roll over the spot and continue on into the hole.

The Three Elements of a Perfect Putt

To hit a perfect, on-line putt, three things have to happen at impact: The path of the putterhead has to be straight along the target line; the putterface has to be square to the target; and contact has to be made on the sweet spot of the putterface. To tell the truth, you can hit the ball on-line without perfect path, face angle, or contact, but it's a much easier game without trying to offset mistakes.

Two things occur if you strike a putt when your path is not straight along the target line. Assuming the face is still square to the target, sidespin is imparted to the ball, just like in the full swing. If the path goes from in to out, the ball will spin slightly from right to left as it rolls, encouraging the ball to go left and slowing it down. When the path is out to in, the ball spins from left to right, and tends to drift weakly to the right.

The other effect a faulty path has on a putt is starting direction. If the path goes to the left, the ball will typically start left. If the path is right, the ball will usually start right—even if the face remains square to the target line. That said, a faulty path probably gets too much credit for most missed putts. Since it's easy to see when your path is off, many players naturally assume that it's the main reason why the ball went off-line. But according to Dave Pelz, *GOLF Magazine*'s Technical and Short Game Consultant, there's a more likely culprit: face angle. A former scientist at NASA, Pelz has conducted exhaustive research on the physics of putting, and one of the many things he has discovered is that only 20 percent of a golfer's error in path is actually transmitted to the golf ball. Translated, that means if the putterhead is moving out to in, five degrees to the left of the target line, the ball will roll only one degree left of the target line, assuming the face is square to the target. That's about two inches on a 20-foot putt. So, a faulty path, while easy to see, has less effect on the ball's direction than you might imagine.

An error in face angle, on the other hand, is difficult to see—especially in somebody else's stroke—but Pelz's research shows that 90 percent of a golfer's error in face angle is transmitted to the golf ball. That means if the face is 10 degrees closed at impact, the ball will go 9 degrees left of the target line—and miss the hole by almost two feet on a 20-foot putt. So, when your putts miss the hole significantly to the right or left, your path may be off, but your face angle almost definitely is.

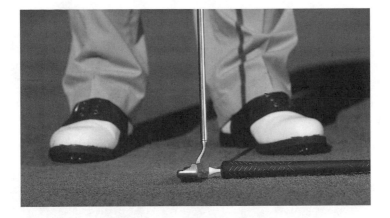

> ### BEST TIP: Hit the Tee
>
> Want to check your face angle at impact? Stick a tee in the end of a grip and lay the club on the green. Pretend the shaft is your target line. Set up to the tee and make your normal stroke: If the face is square, you'll tap the tee solidly; if it's open or closed, you'll knock the club off-line.
>
> —Martin Hall, *GOLF Magazine* Master Teaching Professional

How about the third factor: solid contact? How important is that? First, you should understand what happens when you make contact off the sweet spot. If, for example, you make contact toward the toe of the putter, the heel kicks forward, the face twists open, and less energy is imparted to the ball.

BEST TIP: Band-Aid Cure

Wrap two Band-Aids around the face of the putter so the pads form a half-inch frame of the sweet spot. If you make contact in the middle of the face, the putt will come off as usual. But if you make contact off center, the ball will hit one of the pads and roll about half as far. As solid contact becomes easier, move the Band-Aids closer together.

—Darrell Kestner, *GOLF Magazine*
Top 100 Teacher

Chances are, the putt will finish farther right and shorter than you were expecting. Exactly how much depends on how the putter you're using is constructed, but Pelz found that, on average, an eight-foot putt hit a quarter inch toward the toe will miss the hole 95 percent of the time. Clearly, the farther you get from the hole, the worse the odds get. The putting stroke may be a small motion, but don't take solid contact for granted; it's too important to ignore.

Common Faults

Straight stroke, square face, solid contact—simple, right? Think about it for a second: It's not like you're trying to make a full shoulder turn and drive the legs and clear the hips and finish in balance. It's a simple, pendulum-like motion controlled by the arms and shoulders. Weather and course conditions play a part, but mostly, if you're missing putts it's because you're making mistakes—adding flaws to a simple activity. The physical challenge of putting is less about achieving kinesthetic brilliance than it is avoiding mistakes. Next, we'll cover some of the most common errors and point to solutions.

Make a Stroke with Two Clubs

For a consistent stroke, you must have a feeling of unification between the shoulders, arms, hands, and club. Want to make it easy? Try it the hard way first: With a putter in one hand and a sand wedge in the other, make strokes with both, keeping the clubs parallel and about three inches apart throughout. If you can move both shoulders, arms, hands, and clubs in unison, doing it with one club will be a piece of cake.

Fault

Jerking the putter back away from the ball.

Effect

If the backstroke is rushed or jerky, you can bet something's going to move out of sequence, most likely the hands. That usually means the putterhead will swing off-line, or the putterface will rotate open or closed. As a result, whatever mistakes were made in the backstroke have to be undone in the through-stroke to hit a straight putt. Since the extraneous movement that occurred has to be repeated in reverse, the chances of hitting the ball where you've aimed are slim.

Cure

It can be hard to start the stroke smoothly when the body and club are dead still. The muscles can

A slight forward press often prevents a jerky start.

get "twitchy" and throw the backstroke out of whack. If this is a problem for you, try using a trigger to initiate the stroke. Before starting the putterhead back, tap it gently on the turf or press your hands just slightly toward the hole. Those are just two examples; the point is that setting the body in motion before the stroke makes it much easier to take the putterhead away from the ball smoothly. If you're smooth, you're much more likely to keep the putterface square and on-line. Experiment to find a trigger that works for you.

BEST TIP: Don't Drop the Ball

To keep the putterhead on-line and the putterface square in the backstroke, there can't be any unnecessary movement in the wrists. Try this drill to check your wrists: Assume your normal setup and grip, then have a friend wedge a golf ball between your right wrist and the grip. Stroke the putt. If the ball falls out, your wrists have hinged on the backstroke. Only if the wrists remain still will the ball stay lodged in place.

—Bill Davis, *GOLF Magazine* Top 100 Teacher

Fault

Making an excessively short (or long) backstroke and then having to accelerate (or decelerate) on the forward stroke.

Swing the putter back smoothly with the arms and shoulders.

Effect

The natural putting stroke is like a pendulum—the backstroke should match the through-stroke. Any effort to change that natural motion—like slowing the putterhead down to compensate for an overly long backstroke, or making an very short backstroke then jerking the putterhead through—makes it very difficult to keep the putterface square and to maintain a feel for speed.

Cure

The big misconception when it comes to putting tempo is that you have to *try* to accelerate the put-

Let the natural swinging motion power the through-stroke.

terhead into the ball. You simply don't. Remember, the putterhead comes to a complete stop, however brief, at the top of the backstroke, then starts moving again, which means it's accelerating. Even if you apply no effort at all and just let gravity pull the putterhead through, it will accelerate into the ball. So don't try to control the acceleration of the putter on the through-stroke. Think of the arms, hands, and putter as one unit, and let gravity drive the motion, like a pendulum. If you've made a solid backstroke, the putterhead will naturally swing through on the right line with a square putterface. You'll have a better feel for speed, too: Like a slingshot, the farther back you swing the putter, the faster the ball will roll. In time, you'll develop a feel for how the length of the stroke determines distance.

Fault

Peeking to watch the ball roll.

Effect

Unless your head swivels perfectly, it's almost impossible to move it without somehow moving your body as well, and even the slightest body movement before contact, especially on short putts, can make the difference between a miss and a make. Remember the pendulum: If the tower moves, the pendulum won't swing on the same path. In other words, you'll throw the putterhead off-line.

Cure

Focus not only on watching the ball during the stroke, but also watching the spot the ball occupied after impact is made. Keeping your eyes down ensures that the head—and the body—remains still. On putts over 10 feet, you'll still have enough time

On short putts, keep your eyes down and listen for the ball to drop.

to look up and see the ball roll to the hole. On short putts, keep your head down and listen for the sound of the ball going into the cup.

Fault

Letting the left wrist break down as the putter approaches impact.

Effect

Ideally, the back of the left hand should match the angle of the putterface. If the left wrist hinges before impact, the putterface flips out of position, usually sending the ball left of the target. Left-wrist breakdown usually happens when a putter gets nervous and makes a tentative stroke—almost always on short putts when, for whatever reason, there is a lack of aggression. That's what makes it so frustrating; it usually involves a very makable putt.

Cure

There are two basic ways to attack left-wrist breakdown. One is to resolve to be aggressive, especially on short putts. Hit them firmly, so the ball hits the back of the cup and falls in. Take a look to make sure your backstroke isn't longer than it should be on those short putts. With a shorter backstroke, you can make an aggressive forward stroke without the risk of hitting the ball past the hole.

To cure left-wrist breakdown, keep your backstroke short and make an aggressive through-stroke.

However, resolving to be aggressive on short putts is no cure-all, because what your mind tells your body to do and what your body actually does can often be two different things. And it's not just limited to the average golfer; Tour pros battle left-wrist breakdown all the time. They practice and make resolutions, and see sports psychologists. They change putters. They change caddies. And when none of that works—when their left wrist still makes the occasional ill-timed flip—they change the way they hold the club. At least some do. Fred Couples, Tom Kite, and Karrie Webb, to name a few, all have experimented with or switched to a cross-handed grip, which is much more effective in controlling left-wrist breakdown and its evil cousin, the yips, than a standard reverse-overlap grip.

Fault

"The yips," or convulsive movements of the hand and wrist muscles on short putts.

Effect

The yips often begin with chronic left-wrist breakdown and evolve into a problem rooted more in the mind than the body, ultimately affecting the entire stroke. At their worst, the yips make it almost impossible to draw the putterhead away from the ball without making a flipping motion. They're insidious because they strike seemingly at random and can just as easily disappear, although some of the world's greatest players (Sam Snead and Johnny Miller, among others) spent huge chunks of their careers battling them.

Cure

Two popular remedies for curing the yips are gripping the putter cross-handed and switching to a long putter. The term "cross-handed" implies something quite complicated, but it simply means reversing the hands so the left is below the right on the grip instead of above it. It's also referred to as "left-hand-low," which is not as catchy but might be more appropriate. Whatever you call it, it's a powerful weapon against left-wrist breakdown. Whereas in a standard grip, the lower position of the right hand encourages the left wrist to hinge, the cross-handed grip promotes the opposite—the right hand and arm stabilize the left wrist.

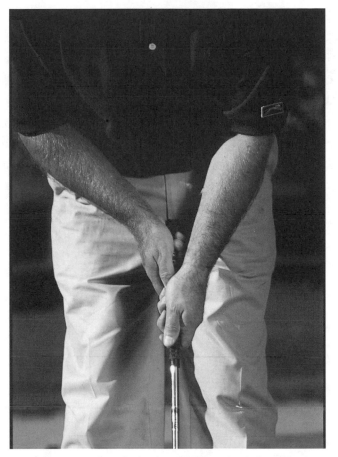

The cross-handed grip stabilizes the left wrist.

There's another big difference between cross-handed and traditional: With a standard grip, the right shoulder is significantly lower than the left at address, because the right hand is below the left on the grip. Reversing the hands realigns the shoulders, which actually makes the stroke more of a true pendulum motion. So, in some ways, it makes more sense to grip the club cross-handed than with a traditional grip.

Start by wrapping all four fingers of the left hand around the club near the bottom of the grip, so there's room for the right hand to go above it. As with a standard grip, the back of the left hand faces the target and the left thumb rests on top of the grip. Place the right hand on the club with the palm facing the target and the thumb slipped under the thumb pad of the left hand. You can hold the club with all the fingers of the right hand, or, if it's more comfortable, lay the right forefinger over the knuckles of the left hand. Overlapping in this manner will bring the hands slightly closer together but comfort is the primary issue.

Your other option, of course, is the long putter. Choosing this recourse, however, also means that you can throw out most of the instruction you've read so far. The long putter, nothing more than a regular putterhead attached to a shaft that is about 50 inches long (standard length for a men's putter is 35 inches), was developed in the early 1990s by Charlie Owens, a Senior PGA Tour player who was looking to fight the effects that age was having on his putting stroke—and to beat the yips.

The long putter has been a savior for many players with "the yips."

Being the first, Owens also had to develop a method for using the long putter. The technique is unusual: Holding the end of the putter with your left hand, you anchor it against the top of your breastbone, or under your chin. In terms of a pendulum, this anchor is the fixed point from which the pendulum swings. The right hand holds on to the club halfway down the shaft. Using light grip

Langer's Solution

Besides winning the Masters, Bernhard Langer is also well known for having a nasty case of the yips. He experimented with just about everything under the sun to beat them, with varying levels of success. One of his most successful experiments was an alternative method of gripping the putter that eliminated any chance of left-wrist breakdown. First, he held the putter below the grip with his left hand, on the shaft of the club. Then, with his right hand, he held the grip against the inside of his left forearm. The result was that the shaft of the putter served as a splint for his left wrist. He had to crouch severely to reach the ball, but there was no chance that his left wrist would hinge.

pressure, you pull the club away from the ball with the right hand, then guide it through by extending the right arm down the target line. The club is so long that it almost swings itself—very little assistance from the right hand is required. As a result, good tempo is easier to achieve and yips are very rare. Plus, the technique produces such a pure pendulum motion that getting a good roll on the ball is virtually guaranteed.

The downside to the long putter is that the length and weight of the club can be hard to control. If you make a mistake in the backstroke with a short putter, there's a chance you might be able to compensate for it on the forward stroke, rerouting the putterhead to where it should be. With the long putter, manipulating the head during

Famous yipper Bernhard Langer developed this strange grip.

the stroke is tough to do. If you make a mistake in the backstroke—like moving the putterhead outside the line—you're basically stuck with it for the rest of the stroke.

BEST TIP: Look at the Hole

Most golfers I've seen suffer from the yips have a problem with peeking—looking up at the hole just before contact—which throws the putter-head off-line. Unfortunately, telling them not to peek is like telling them not to think of pink elephants. Instead, I tell yippers to look at the hole throughout the stroke, even when they play. Not only does it eliminate peeking, but taking your eyes off the ball helps you relax and stroke it smoothly.

—John Gerring, *GOLF Magazine*
Top 100 Teacher

Strategy

Good technique gives you the potential to be a good putter, but to reach that potential you have to put it all together on the golf course. It's the difference between making a good stroke and actually *putting well*, which requires a set of perceptive eyes, intelligent strategy, and a fair dose of mental toughness. Applying what you know is the fun part; it's actually playing the chess match after learning how to move each piece. And on the course is where you have the most to learn, no matter your level of play.

The rules for putting, one might say, are much more universal than the rules for putting technique, so you must abide by them. For example, if the green is sloped from right to left, the putt is go-

Good putting requires perceptive eyes, smart strategy, and guts.

ing to break to the left, whether you use a reverse-overlap or a cross-handed grip; if you're putting against the grain on Bermudagrass greens, the ball will roll slower than usual. Regardless of your technique, you've got no chance of making putts if you don't recognize such on-course factors.

But there is more. You need a putter that suits you, something you can feel comfortable with as you stand over the ball. You need to know how to practice, so you can maintain your stroke and ensure that your putter remains your friend, not your enemy. That's what the remainder of this book is all about: getting out of the theoretical, and getting into the practical.

The Mental Side?

The old saying is that golf is "90 percent mental," but it's one of the more misunderstood truths in the game. Most folks associate the mental side with confidence, and confidence with emotional strength. That's part of it, but what people don't pay much attention to is how that confidence is developed. It's looked upon as a sort of magical quality that arbitrarily attaches itself to a lucky someone. You hear stories of Tour players seeing sports psychologists in an effort to regain their confidence, which may give the impression to the average golfer that these gurus have a unique insight into what must be a complicated process. Okay, for the pros, maybe confidence is a bit complex. They're the best players in the world, and they're playing for millions of dollars, not to mention their livelihood. But for the rest of us, the primary source of confidence is simple: It comes from having a specific plan, standing over a putt with no questions in your mind. You know how much the putt will break and how fast the green is, and you know your stroke is solid. The questions—or worries— aren't there because you've taken care of business. You've read the putt correctly, you've gauged the speed of the green, and you've spent enough time practicing to feel good about your mechanics. You're confident, but there's nothing magical about it. It comes from being smart and prepared.

The preparation part is simple: practice, practice, practice (see Chapter Four). But how do you get the smarts? There's a wealth of strategic knowledge to be had, from recognizing undulations to understanding the effect of different grass conditions. It's not the kind of knowledge that can simply be absorbed through reading; much of it comes from experience. Consider this chapter, then, as your guide.

Reading Greens

Put simply, most greens are sloped in some way, which affects how the ball will roll. Reading a green means identifying what slopes exist between your ball and the hole, then determining how the line

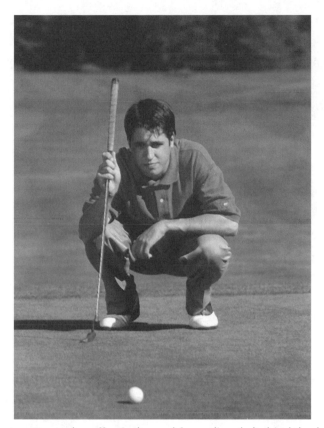

Most putts can be effectively read from directly behind the ball.

and speed will be affected by them. Despite the pains you see the pros taking on television, reading a green is not that complicated. Standing a few feet directly behind your ball, crouch down and survey the terrain between your ball and the cup. From there you should be able to see what slopes exist. If the green is sloped to the left, the putt will curve, or break, to the left, so you must aim to the right of the hole to compensate. If the green is sloped to the right, the ball will break to the right, so aim left. How far outside the hole do you aim? It depends on how angled the slope is, for one, and how hard you plan to hit the ball. You might be able to read the slopes in a green the first time you play, but knowing how much a putt will break comes with experience. The more you play, the better your green-reading skills will become.

You don't have to rely solely on crouching behind the ball to read the slope in a green, although if that angle seems to give you a conclusive view, there's little need to gather more information. But greens are usually sloped in several ways, so many putts will have more than one break in them. If crouching behind the ball still leaves you with questions in your mind, check the line from behind the hole. Sometimes getting a reverse angle can reveal things you didn't see from behind the ball.

And, as long as you're walking the length of the putt anyway, looking at the line from the side can reveal hidden upslopes or downslopes that will affect the roll of the ball. If you're still not sure, remember that your eyes can fool you, but your feet can't. You can feel when you're not walking on a flat surface, so pay attention as you walk along the line of your putt. However, don't get carried away with reading greens. Most of the time, the first impression you get when you crouch behind the ball is correct; if you continually second-guess yourself and check all the angles, your pace of play will be unbearably slow.

Every Putt Is Straight

Don't ever compensate for a slope in the green by altering your stroke. Even if there are six feet of break, play it straight. That is, pick a secondary target—in this case, a spot six feet outside the hole—and go about your business as if that spot were the hole, and you're about to hit a straight putt. Aim the putterface at the secondary target, align your body to the putterface, and make a straight-back, straight-through stroke along the target line that extends from the ball to the secondary target. Your alignment, not your stroke, allows for the break. If you've read the putt correctly, the slope will take care of bringing the ball down to the hole.

Play breaking putts just like straight ones, only adjust your aim.

The Linchpin: Speed

Every time you read a slope in a green, how much break you play—how far outside the hole you aim—depends on how fast you intend to hit the ball. This is especially true for short putts. A simple example: You're faced with a seven-foot putt, slightly downhill and sloped from right to left. If you hit the putt softly, so it would fall into the hole on its last rotation, you'd aim maybe four inches to the right so the slope could bring it back. But with the ball rolling that slowly, it's more likely to be thrown off-line by whatever imperfections exist on the green. So do you have to play that much break? Not at all. You could aim at the right edge of the cup instead of four inches outside it and still make the putt—but you'd have to hit the ball much harder. This presents some potential problems: If the ball doesn't hit the cup in exactly the right spot, it won't go in; and if it misses the cup altogether, it'll roll way past, maybe leaving you an even longer putt coming back.

So what's the happy medium? According to Pelz, it's 17 inches. He has found that a putt has the best chance to go in if it's hit hard enough to roll 17 inches past the hole. No more, no less. That's fast enough to resist most of a green's imperfections, yet slow enough that it will fall into the cup even if it isn't dead-center.

The challenge, then, is twofold: Being able to "read" speed in a green, and then, being able to dial in the right stroke. There are a few factors that influence how fast the ball will roll. First is the height of the grass on the green; the closer it is shaved, the faster the ball will roll. However, it's nearly impos-

Hitting short putts firmly takes away break, but if you miss . . .

sible to tell just by looking. Your best bet is to hit a few putts on the practice green before you play; it should reflect the speed of all the greens on the course.

The second is the incline or decline of the green. Obviously, a putt going downhill will be faster than one headed uphill. Most of the time these slopes are pretty apparent as you stand on the green. However, if the golf course itself is built on fairly uneven terrain, some slopes aren't so obvious. That's why it's smart to start reading the greens before you get to them. As you walk or ride up the fairway, pay attention to the overall slope of the green and the surrounding area. Is the entire green pitched in a certain direction? If so, you can bet the ball will tend to roll that way.

An Uphill Battle

Your ball's heading straight for the hole, about to drop in, but then curls away at the last moment and misses. Blame the golf gods if you want, but Pelz blames "the lumpy doughnut." During the course of a day, the average green is crushed by thousands of footprints that depress the grass everywhere except within a few inches of the hole, where nobody steps. So the hole and a small circle around it are slightly raised, meaning the ball has to go up a tiny ramp the last six inches or so to the hole, exactly when it's moving the slowest. The upshot: You can make a perfect read and a seemingly perfect stroke, and still miss the putt. That's one reason you need a little speed on the putt as it approaches the hole.

> ### BEST TIP: The Lower Half
>
> The best perspective for reading a long putt is halfway along the line on the low side. Assessing the putt from the halfway point gives a good feel for the overall distance, and the low side reveals any rise or fall. Keep in mind, distance is the key on long putts. Reading putts from behind the ball is more important from short range, where the break should be your primary concern.
>
> —Jim Flick, *GOLF Magazine*
> Master Teaching Professional

Another factor that influences a putt's speed is grain. Grain refers to the direction the grass grows on the green: A ball rolling with the grain will be faster than a ball rolling against it. Look for drainage patterns on the greens to determine the direction of the grain. If there's a water hazard around the green, the grain will usually run toward it. If the green is cut into a hill or mountain, the grain will tend to run down the slope, even if the undulations in the green appear different. On flat greens, the grain usually grows toward the setting sun. If you're looking at the green and the grain is running away from you, the grass will appear shiny; if the grain is coming toward you, it has a duller look. In some circumstances, grain can affect the break of the putt but for the most part, its impact is on the speed.

Once you've taken into account all the factors that can affect the speed of a putt, you're faced with the second part of the equation: How to make the proper adjustments in your stroke. How big a stroke do you have to make? How hard do you have to hit the ball so it has enough speed to reach, even roll past, the hole? Unfortunately, the answer to this one is not so black and white. It's a question of feel—an instinctive communication from your eyes, which take in all the visual information just discussed, to your brain,

The Amateur Side

If you're unfamiliar with the expression "never up, never in," it means that a putt that finishes short of the hole never had a chance to go in. Simple enough. But there's a similar philosophy to breaking putts: If the ball goes past the hole on the low side, it likewise never had a chance to drop. This, unfortunately, is a typical amateur mistake; you have to play away from the hole on a breaking putt and hit the ball a little harder, which can be hard to make yourself do. That's why the low side of the cup on a breaking putt is known as "the amateur side." But consider that a ball rolling on the high, or "pro," side of the cup—even if you've played too much break—always has a chance to hit something or lose speed and fall in. But once the ball is rolling below the hole, nothing can make it go back up the slope.

which processes the information, and finally, to your body, which makes a stroke based on what the brain tells it. Perfecting those lines of communication comes with practice and repetition: After you've done it enough, your body knows how to make a putt roll three feet or 30 without reinventing the wheel.

On long putts, make your stroke longer, not quicker.

One thing is for certain: You'll find it easier to gauge speed if your tempo is consistent from stroke to stroke. Tempo is the relationship between the pace of your backstroke and the pace of your through-stroke. If you swing the putterhead back very slowly then jerk it through, your tempo is uneven. If you take it back quickly and decelerate

Try to make your backstroke and through-stroke at the same pace.

going through, you're in no better shape. Strive for a smooth, even tempo, where the putterhead moves away from the ball slowly, then swings through at what feels to be the same pace, like a free-swinging pendulum.

Then maintain that tempo on all putts. If the putt is long, don't quicken the stroke, just lengthen it. On shorter putts, make a shorter stroke with the same tempo. You'll have a better feel for different speeds if your tempo is consistent. If the tempo changes from one stroke to the next, it's just another variable to complicate the equation.

Strategizing: Short Putts

In a nutshell, putts of about eight feet and less are why so many golfers hate putting. They look easy, they *should be* easy, but somehow they're frightening propositions. Maybe it's because they are easier to miss than they are to make. And not just for weekend golfers: Pelz's research shows that, on average, even the best putters on the PGA Tour make less than 60 percent of the six-footers they face. Remember, that's on average: When they shoot low scores, you can bet they're doing better than 60 percent. With this in mind, you shouldn't expect to be flawless from close range, but you should also recognize that improving your short putting is probably the first thing to do if you're looking to cut strokes.

Essentially, good short putting is about making a sound stroke despite your nerves. Alignment is important on any putt, of course, but it's the key on short putts, as you expect to roll them perfectly on-line. From inside six feet, you'll rarely have to aim more than a ball's width outside the cup. If you miss, it's usually because of a mechanical glitch that caused you to open or close the putterface, move your head or body, or make contact off the sweet spot. You can guard against these breakdowns by practicing and perfecting your mechanics on the practice green. That's taking care of the physical side of things. To take care of the mental side, a preputt routine is a big help.

A preputt routine is exactly that: a specific ritual you go through before every putt. For example, crouch behind the ball, read the break of the putt, and pick an intermediate target along the line. Walk to the side of the ball and make a practice stroke or two, sensing the effort required. Set the putterhead behind the ball, aligning it to your intermediate target. Take your grip, then align your body so it's parallel to the target line. Swivel your head to look at the hole, swivel your head back to the ball, then make your stroke. That's a preputt routine. Doing it

First, square the putterface to your intended line.

before every putt breeds familiarity and consistency and helps establish a rhythm. Plus, it's great on short putts because it gives you a chance to focus on something else besides your nerves and all the things that could go wrong. Develop your own preputt routine (the one above is just a good example) and discipline

With the face square, take your grip and align your body.

yourself to complete it before every putt, long or short. If you can repeat a good routine, you have a better chance of repeating a good stroke, too.

You also have to take a different approach to a short putt's line and speed. For instance, you're facing a left-to-right four-footer that reads like you should aim the ball outside the left edge. "Don't give the hole away" is an expression you'll hear from experienced golfers, which means don't aim outside the parameters of the hole if it isn't necessary. On this particular four-footer, you could aim at the left side of the hole instead of outside the edge; you'd just have to hit the ball a little harder.

For better players, this is not a bad idea. Since the ball is so close to the hole, more precise targeting is possible, and it's often easier to make a smooth, confident stroke when the target is inside, instead of outside, the hole. For most golfers, however, taking on a more aggressive strategy for short putts can wreak havoc with the stroke, throwing off tempo. It all depends on how confident you feel over the short ones.

BEST TIP: Head Still

To train yourself to keep your head and body still during the stroke, make practice strokes with the top of your head against a wall. With the head forced to remain still, the body will do the same, and you'll get a feeling for controlling the stroke with only the arms and shoulders. Try to reproduce this feeling on the golf course.

—Darrell Kestner, *GOLF Magazine*
Top 100 Teacher

Strategizing: Long Putts

Putts of 30 feet and longer aren't nearly as nerve-wracking as short putts since you don't have any real expectations of making them. Unfortunately, this attitude most often leads to a lack of concentration, which is a big mistake; it takes as much precision to hit a 30-footer within a few feet of the hole as it does to drain a five-footer. Another thing to remember is that if you're consistently facing knee-knockers for your second putts, you're often going to find yourself three-putting—the cardinal sin. The average golfer could cut three to five strokes a round just by eliminating three-putts. In other words, the ability to hit long putts close to the hole is a great scoring tool.

The key to long putts, also known as lag putts, is distance and therefore speed. Line is less of an issue because your target is wider, as your goal is to leave the ball within a couple feet of the hole. Nevertheless, on lag putts, most amateurs focus too intently on the line and so tend to make many more mistakes in distance. To gauge the proper speed, make several practice strokes to help your body adjust to the distance. Then, go through your normal preputt routine of reading the line and aligning the putterface then your body. During the stroke, stick to your same smooth, even tempo. You'll be surprised how good your feel is for distance if your tempo is consistent.

BEST TIP: Use a Mini-Swing on Long Putts

Controlling the speed of the ball on long putts is much easier when you make a long, smooth backstroke—like the mini-swing of a chip shot. If the putt is extra long—more than 50 feet— don't fight the feeling that you have to hit the ball hard. Allow for a little play in the wrists; you'll be able to generate more swing speed while still staying relaxed. If the longer stroke causes your body to move slightly, let it. The less tension you have, the better your tempo, and the better your touch.

—Brad Faxon, 6-time
Winner on the PGA Tour

No matter how good you are at lag putting, you can't always count on being left with a tap-in. So you have to consider the best place—and the worst place—for your next putt. Take the time to analyze the slopes around the hole. If at all possible, you want to be left with a straight, flat putt. If not, straight and uphill is the next best option. In general, uphill putts are easier than downhillers, so take that into account. Also, be aware of what type of break is more comfortable for you. Most right-handed golfers find right-to-left putts easier than left-to-righters. Favor the side of the hole that leaves you in your comfort zone. And if you roll the ball well past the hole, don't turn away in disgust. Watch the ball carefully; it's giving you a free read of your next putt.

Watch your ball roll past for a free read of your next putt.

Tiered Greens

Multilevel, or tiered, greens—those with two or more "shelves" connected by steep slopes—present a unique challenge on long putts. If your ball is on one level and the hole is on another, you basically have three reads to make: the break of the green on the level you're on; how the connecting slope will affect the roll; and the break on the level of the hole. With multiple angles to consider, it's easy to get confused about how the hills are going to affect the putt. But keep in mind that whether the putt is going down to a lower level or up to a higher level, the effect of the slope will always be to pull the ball down the hill. The ball likes going downhill, and will sometimes even reverse direction to do so. It sounds obvious, but when you're analyzing the slopes on tiered greens, it's a helpful thing to remember.

The good news is that most tiered greens are built the same way. Usually, from front to back, the lower level feeds into a slope that rises to an upper level, which is generally pretty flat. This hill profile means that if you're putting down from the upper level, usually all you have to do is hit the ball hard enough so it reaches the downslope. There are always exceptions, but more often than not, the slope will give the ball plenty of momentum to reach hole locations on the lower level.

Going up the slope to a higher level is usually a tougher putt. The ball has to roll significantly faster than normal to get up the hill, and it can be hard to convince your body to make such a long stroke. But if you don't hit the ball hard enough to reach the upper level, it might roll right back and leave you with a second putt longer than your first. At the same time, you can't just whack the ball; the upper level on tiered greens tends to be a bit quicker, as it's flatter. Too much speed and your ball will roll off the back and then you really have a tough play.

If you're having trouble gauging the proper speed, try tricking yourself into hitting it harder. Ignore the shelf, then imagine that the hole is about 10 feet farther back than it actually is. Gauge the length of your stroke as if you're hitting a straight uphill putt to the imaginary hole farther away. That should give the ball just enough momentum to roll up the hill without rolling over the green.

Different Speeds

Depending on how many different courses you play, you're likely to encounter a variety of greens,

When putting to a top tier, aim for an imaginary Hole
10 feet farther away.

some faster and some slower. To be a consistent
scorer, then, you have to know how to handle
greens of different speeds. The biggest key is not to
get taken by surprise. Always take the time to hit a

few putts on the practice green before the round, and ask your playing partners or the club pro if the speed of the practice green reflects the speed of the greens on the course. Usually, it will. Make any necessary adjustments on the practice green: a shorter stroke if the green is fast and a longer stroke if it's slow, never changing that smooth-back, smooth-through tempo. You'll adapt to the speed of the greens much more quickly if you don't have to adjust to a change in tempo.

A couple of things to keep in mind. Assuming that the greens are fast because they're well manicured and cut very short (rather than just baked-out hardpan), the ball will tend to break a little bit more. You'll notice this as you warm up. On the course, let the speed of the greens work for you. On most short putts—especially downhillers—all you usually have to do is get the ball rolling for it to reach the hole. That takes some of the guesswork out of speed control, allowing you to focus less on making the perfect stroke and more on finding the right line. Fast greens are usually pretty true, so if you get the ball rolling on line, it should behave as you expect it to.

Slow greens work exactly the opposite way: Whatever speed the ball gets, it's getting from

On fast greens, just get downhill putts started.

you—the green isn't going to help at all. On the other hand, slow greens also tend to break less. They can be very easy to score on once you get used to the speed because so many of the putts are straight (even if they look slightly sloped). Keep the green-reading simple and maintain a smooth stroke, focusing on consistent tempo.

> ### *BEST TIP: Choke Down on Slippery Putts*
>
> Golfers sometimes control speed on downhill putts by striking the ball out on the toe of the putterface. It kills power at impact but also causes the putterhead to twist. Here's a better way to take speed off a fast putt: Make some regular practice strokes, then bend over and choke down on the handle until your hands are almost at the metal. Then execute a normal stroke, making contact on the sweet spot. By shortening the putter, you decrease power, without the risk of the face twisting off-line.
>
> —Dave Pelz, *GOLF Magazine*
> Technical and Short Game Consultant

Types of Grasses

Golf course agronomy is pretty complicated stuff, with all sorts of different grasses at the course designer's disposal, each with different characteristics based on climate and resistance to certain weeds. Luckily, not all of them have significantly different playing qualities; what a nightmare that would be for the golfer. As it is, there are essentially three different types of grasses you need to be aware of: bentgrass, Bermudagrass, and ryegrass.

Bentgrass has traditionally been reserved for courses in four-season climates, because it doesn't stand up well to extreme heat. If maintained carefully (it requires a lot of attention), bentgrass can be very lush; the grain grows very tightly and can be cut very short, so most of the fastest greens you'll see are bentgrass. It's usually found in the northern part of the country, but recent advancements in cultivation and maintenance techniques have allowed more courses in the South to install bentgrass greens.

Bermudagrass requires less maintenance and handles extreme heat much better than bent, so it's prevalent in desert or tropical climates. However, since it doesn't grow as tightly and can't be cut as short, it's hard to make Bermudagrass greens as fast as bentgrass greens. Because the individual blades are longer, grain is much more of a factor when putting on Bermuda greens. Not only will grain affect the speed of your putts, it can also contribute to the break. Putts going with the grain often break more; those going against the grain break less. It usually takes a round or two to get used to these differences if you normally play on bentgrass.

Ryegrass greens are far less common than bent or Bermuda. Rye is generally not the primary grass on a course, but is often used during the winter months in a process called "overseeding." In the desert of Palm Springs, for example, winter mornings often leave a thin layer of frost on the greens. The Bermudagrass that holds up so well to the blistering summer heat doesn't like the cold at all, so many of the courses in the area overseed with ryegrass in the fall. Its playing characteristics lie somewhere in the middle. It can be cut shorter than Bermuda, but the grain isn't very consistent, so the surface generally isn't as true as bentgrass greens.

Weather Considerations

In Scotland, wind and rain are almost a daily event on the golf course. In the U.S., inclement weather is less frequent—and golfers are less willing to endure it—but sometimes you have no choice. There are a few things to keep in mind.

When it comes to your putting, light rain is mostly just annoying; it shouldn't interfere with the short, simple motion of your stroke. Your main concern should be to keep the ball and the face of your putter as dry as possible, to ensure normal contact. However, rain makes the greens wet, and that can require some adjustments on your part. If the greens are slightly damp, they'll just be a little

From Off the Green

The putter doesn't have to be restricted to use on the green. From the fringe, or even from a greenside bunker, the putter can be a valuable weapon. But the conditions have to be right. Unless you're right on the edge of the fringe, make sure the grass isn't too much longer than the green and the ground is level. If the conditions are going to significantly slow down your ball or possibly kick it off-line, it's better to chip.

Putting from a greenside bunker is only a viable option if the lip of the bunker is very low, allowing the ball to roll out without jumping into the air. There shouldn't be any more than a few feet of rough between the bunker and the green, and make sure the sand is firm. Remember, don't touch the putterhead to the sand at address—that's a Rules violation.

Putting from the fringe is fine, as long as you can judge the roll.

When the wind is up, widen your stance for stability.

slower. But if water is accumulating, your ball will have a tendency to skid off the face of the putter, hydroplaning on top of a thin layer of water, like a car on a wet road. This could send the ball off-line slightly, especially if contact is made off the sweet spot. Once the ball stops skidding and makes contact with the grass, it will slow down considerably. With the water providing resistance, the ball will also break less than usual. Nevertheless, since most of your putts will be playing slower and straighter, wet greens give you an opportunity to make more aggressive strokes. Keep that benefit in mind.

Wind, on the other hand, can have a very definite effect on your stroke: It can blow you off balance. If you're feeling unstable, widen your stance slightly, so your feet are shoulder-width apart or even wider; this will help anchor you to the ground. Even then, making your normal stroke on a windy day requires a little extra concentration. In your preputt routine, focus on making a smooth practice stroke with an even tempo. And take your time; don't let the wind rush you into hitting the putt before you're ready or with a quicker pace.

In extreme circumstances, wind can affect the break of a putt. Your ball will never be blown wildly off-line unless the playing conditions are, well, unplayable. But when the breeze is blowing at 20 mph or better, wind's influence on a putt is similar to the effect of grain. Downwind putts will be faster; upwind will be slower. If the wind blows with the break, play the ball a little farther outside the hole; if the wind blows against the break, play it

closer. If you find yourself with a downhill, downwind, downgrain putt: Hit it lightly. Then hope.

One final point: Wind also acts as a drying agent.
If you're playing on a damp course, and the wind
picks up, expect the greens to dry out. And dry,
windblown greens tend to be fast.

Practice

For those of you who are fed up with the constant reminders in golf books and magazines that you can't improve without practice, here's the bad news: Not only do you have to practice regularly to improve, but your putting will quickly deteriorate without it. How much you know about making a good stroke is unimportant. You have to constantly reinforce the muscle memory that produces the precise pendulum motion of the putting stroke. And even if your mechanics are excellent, without practice you'll have a hard time gauging speed, and your stroke will have a tendency to break down in pressure situations. If your mechanics aren't perfect, practice is the one chance you have to make corrections; an actual round of golf is not the time to tinker with your stroke.

So you have to practice. (Yawn.) But here's the good news: Hitting a putt may not be as exciting as hitting a drive, but practicing putting can be much more fun than pounding tee shots. Drills, games, competitions—there's a host of things you can do to improve on the green aside from standing in one place and hitting putt after putt after putt. It's easy for the mind to wander while you're beating balls on the driving range; on the other hand, if you plan your putting practice sessions wisely, there's no reason to ever get bored on the practice green.

Setting Goals

"Practice with a purpose" is another time-worn cliché. Nevertheless, if putting practice has a reputation for being tedious, it's because most people do it aimlessly, just going from hole to hole and quickly losing interest. It's a much more engaging activity if you're actually trying to accomplish something, so set a goal for yourself before each session. Think about your tendencies and choose a daily objective; for example, working on lag putting by hitting a certain number of 30-footers within a six-foot circle around the hole. With a goal, you can track your progress along the way, which keeps things more interesting.

Set goals when you practice, such as trying to make 10 four-footers in a row.

Once you have a goal, don't put pressure on yourself to practice until your back goes out. Is there anyone who wouldn't go a little crazy from spending two hours straight just working on, say, stroke mechanics? Even with multiple goals, two hours is overdoing it. If you need work on short putts and big breakers, for instance, try to break the practice up over a couple of days. Stick to one goal per session and keep the sessions short—half an hour is plenty of time if you work steadily. Ultimately, you'll retain more information if you stay fresh throughout the session.

BEST TIP: Diagnose Your Stroke

The putts just aren't dropping for you lately, but you don't know why. To find the answer, buy 15 feet of yellow string and two 10-inch gutter spikes (about the cost of a Sunday paper). Attach the string to the spikes and find a flat portion of the practice green. Stick one spike about 17 inches behind the middle of the hole, then stretch the cord taut and spike the other in the green. The string should be about four inches above the ground. Hit putts, using the string as a guide to be sure the putterhead is moving straight back and through. If it is and the ball is starting right or left of the string, the putterface is opening or closing at impact. You can check your speed, too: If the ball misses, it should finish even with the far spike, 17 inches past the hole.

—Kent Cayce, *GOLF Magazine*
Top 100 Teacher

Working on Mechanics

If you're consistently missing makable putts, you might want to brush up on your mechanics. Bad habits can creep into your stroke like weeds, causing problems without you knowing it.

Maybe there's some hidden flaw in your stroke that only the trained eye of a golf professional can uncover. But before you jump to that conclusion, spend a practice session checking and working on your alignment, putterhead path, and face angle. It may be that refamiliarizing yourself with the fundamentals is all you need to get back on track.

Practicing mechanics is easier than working on anything else, because you don't need a hole, or even a ball. There are dozens of simple things you can do, from practicing a straight stroke against the line of the fringe to checking your alignment at home in a mirror. But the most complete way to monitor your mechanics is to use a practice station.

It's similar to laying down clubs on the range: Find a flat portion of the practice green and drop a ball eight to 10 feet from a hole. If you can, snap a chalk line from the ball to the hole; this is the target line. Put the putterhead behind the ball so the face is square to the target line, then mark this position with two tees, one a quarter inch outside the toe of the putterhead, the other a quarter inch outside the heel. Then create two rows of tees on either side of the target line (including the two marking the putterface) to guide the putterhead on a straight-back, straight-through path. The track may have to be slightly rounded to accommodate the shape of your stroke.

Putting with a Range Ball

Do you wonder whether you're making pure contact with the ball? You can find out simply by hitting straight 10-foot putts with a range ball. Align the stripe on the ball so it points down the target line, then make your normal stroke. If the stripe looks like a solid line as the ball rolls to the cup, you've made perfect contact and haven't imparted any sidespin. But if the stripe wobbles, it's an indication of sidespin, and you either cut across the ball or your putterface wasn't square at impact.

Practice with a range ball and make sure the stripe doesn't wobble.

Create a track with tees to check your path and face angle.

Start by making practice strokes without a ball to get a feel for a square putterface and proper path. Then put a ball down and hit a dozen or so putts to the hole. Make whatever adjustments are necessary to roll the ball down the target line and make it drop. If the putterhead doesn't hit the tees during the stroke, your path is essentially straight. If the ball still isn't going in, it's because the putterface isn't square at impact. Stick with the practice station until you make six or seven putts in a row. Then end the session by hitting a handful of putts with no alignment aids, trying to retain the feeling you had while working at the practice station.

Short Putts

What's the point of practicing putts of less than five feet? You may miss them on the course occasionally, but they don't even hold your attention on the practice green. So why bother? It's a good point, actually—there isn't much to be gained from spending a lot of time on something that isn't challenging. But ask yourself: Why are short putts challenging on the course? Because there's pressure—after all, you could always miss and cost yourself a precious stroke. That pressure gets to your nerves, and if your nerves get the better of you, they disrupt your mechanics.

In practicing short putts, your goal should be to strengthen your nerves. This means that you have to create pressure situations for yourself. For example, you could vow not to leave the putting green until you've made 15 three-footers in a row. Use only one ball. Every time you miss, start the count over. You can bet by the time you get to 10 in a row, your nerves will start to kick in. Want to crank the pressure up even more? Make a wager with a friend: First one to sink 15 wins. The extra competition raises the stakes, and the higher the stakes, the higher the pressure.

Long Putts

Practicing from long range means practicing distance control; direction is secondary. So your first priority should be to stroke every putt with a smooth, even tempo. Don't worry about making your mechanics flawless, focus on speed instead. To make sure you develop an overall feel for speed and not just a feel for one particular putt, move around the green as you practice. Spend as much time hitting putts up and down hills as you do in flat areas. To keep you challenged, going from hole to hole can be helpful, but add a little twist to make sure it stays interesting. Dave Pelz invented a game called "Safety Drawback" that is perfect for working on speed control.

The goal is to hit every putt, regardless of distance, either in the hole or so it finishes within a "Safe Zone" around the cup. Seventeen inches past the hole indicates perfect speed, but give yourself a little more room with the Safe Zone. Imagine a circle around the cup with a 34-inch radius. Now, since a putt that finishes short of the hole never has a chance to go in, slice off the half of the circle that is in front of the hole. You're left with a semicircle that begins at the hole an extends 34 inches to the sides and behind it. That's the Safe Zone.

To play the game, start by hitting a lag putt of 20 feet or more. If it finishes within the Safe Zone, you may tap it in. (To measure 34 inches, use the shaft of your putter—most are 35 inches long). If the ball finishes short of the hole or otherwise outside the Safe Zone, you must pull the ball back away from the hole another putter length. So, if you rolled the ball four feet past, you have to pull it away from the hole about three more feet and try to make a seven-foot putt. The same rules apply for the second putt: Leave it outside the Safe Zone, and you have to pull it back again. This game forces you to focus on the proper speed, or you could spend all day at one hole.

Play a game called "Safety Drawback" to test your distance control.

There are variations, as well. If you're working on really long putts—more than 40 feet—you can enlarge the Safe Zone to a full circle, so any putt that finishes within 34 inches of the hole, in any direction, is acceptable. Again, a little competition applies the heat and makes the game more interesting.

BEST TIP: Putt With Your Eyes Closed

During practice, I sometimes putt with my eyes closed, then guess where the ball will finish. Only after the ball stops rolling do I open my eyes to see if I'm right. This drill teaches you to have a better feel for the stroke and what the putterface is doing as it makes contact.

—Greg Norman, 2-time
British Open Champion

Breaking Putts

As with long putts, it's important to vary your practice with breaking putts. You don't want to just groove your stroke to one particular left-to-right 10-footer. You want to become skilled at the process of handling breaking putts, which means reading the line, gauging the speed, choosing a secondary target, and making a straight-back, straight-through stroke. That doesn't mean you have to crouch behind the ball and line up every putt on the practice green (although going through your preputt routine every few strokes is a good idea), but try to keep the putts as fresh as possible. Don't spend too much time on any one putt, and vary your distances between five and 20 feet. If left-to-right putts traditionally give you the most problems, focus on them during the session, but don't ignore right-to-lefters completely. Balancing the two protects the integrity of your mechanics, so you don't get used to making a stroke grooved on only one type of break.

Grooving Tempo

Because good tempo is so closely associated with speed control, practicing long putts is a great way to work on your tempo. Plus, it's easier to get a feel for the putterhead moving back and through at the same pace if you're making a longer stroke. To start, don't pay much attention to distance or direction, just hit a handful of putts from 20 feet or more, working with a light grip pressure and the sense that the putter is moving smoothly and evenly back and

BEST TIP: *Four Corners*

Stick four tees around a hole in the shape of a diamond, with each tee four to five feet from the cup. Use an area with some slope, so that putts from opposite sides of the hole feature opposite breaks.

Stroke three putts from one tee, then rotate to the next station and putt three from there, and so on. The objective is to make 12 putts in a row, three from each tee. If you miss, start over from where you are. If making 12 consecutive putts seems too tough for you, try sinking two at each station.

This drill makes for great practice because you eventually have to make pressure putts from all four stations, each of which features a different break and speed. Don't quit before you meet your objective.

—Karrie Webb, Winner of 17 LPGA Tour Events

through. As you stroke the ball, try saying the words to yourself slowly: "back . . . and . . . through."

Still having a hard time finding the rhythm? Try practicing with headphones on, listening to some steady, soothing music that you like. Or use a metronome if you have one. The beat of the music or the steady "tick-tock" of the metronome will encourage you to keep things on an even keel, without any sudden increases or decreases in speed.

BEST TIP: The Putting Ladder

Here's a great drill to help you regain a feel for distance and stop three-putting. Standing on one side of the practice green, pick a spot just short of the fringe on the other side. Putt a ball as close as you can to that spot without rolling it into the fringe. Putt a second ball as close as possible to the first one without going past it. See how many balls you can roll between the fringe and a point eight feet back, each putt shorter than the one before (see photo at right). You're in mid-season form if you can stop six balls within the eight-foot "ladder."

—Mike Bender, *GOLF Magazine*
Top 100 Teacher

Getting off the Three-Putt Train

Nothing adds more unnecessary strokes to your score than three-putting. If it happens to you more than twice a round, it's definitely something you should address in your practice sessions. Most likely, you're having trouble getting your long putts close to the hole. You're probably leaving yourself

with second putts of five feet or longer, and missing a few of those in a row can really do damage to your confidence. That feeling carries over to the next short putt you have, and suddenly, even if you hit the ball close, two-putting is no guarantee.

So, distance control and confidence are the main areas you should focus on to curb your three-putting. Try working on them together. Spend ten minutes working on three-footers, doing the 15-in-a-row drill to boost your confidence. Then play 18 holes of the Safety Drawback game just discussed, choosing first putts of at least 20 feet each time. That way, you hit a short putt after every long putt, just the way you do on the course. Keep score; par is 36. If you score under 38, you're doing very well.

The Value of Friends

Putting practice is always easier and more enjoyable if you have somebody to do it with. Not only does a partner provide competition for whatever putting drills and contests you devise, but also a second set of eyes. This is especially helpful with alignment; it's fairly easy to be sure the putterface is square at address, but a partner has a much better view of the alignment of your feet, knees, hips, and shoulders relative to the target line. He or she also may spot some flaws in your setup and stroke.

However, don't put too much stock in what your friend says about your mechanics unless he or she is a PGA professional. The first thing that average golfers see when they watch other golfers' strokes is

Have a friend check your setup, especially your alignment.

Play 11

Here's a simple yet challenging game to play with a friend: Go from hole to hole on the practice green, choosing putts of various distances and breaks. On each hole, the player whose first putt finishes closest to the hole gets one point. If a player three-putts, his opponent receives a point. Sinking the first putt earns three points. The first player to reach 11 points wins. Want to go a step further? Play with two balls each, and go to 21. Because points are awarded for lag putting and three-putts, there's pressure on all parts of your putting game.

the path of the putterhead, because it's the most visible part of the stroke. They'll tell you that you missed a putt left because you pulled it, but they can't see if you closed the putterface at impact or made contact on the heel, both of which can also make the ball go left. So they won't tell you all you need to know, and maybe not even the main cause of your misses. Nevertheless, a quick critique can be helpful; just know who it's coming from.

Warming Up Before a Round

Here's a riddle: When are you on the practice green, hitting putts, but not practicing? During the preround warm-up, which may look like practice but is actually something quite different. Practice is a time to work out the kinks in your stroke, to focus on your weaknesses, and sometimes, to take a step back before taking two steps forward. But 20 minutes before you tee off is no time to be thinking anything but positive thoughts. The purpose of the warm-up is not to fix anything; it's to make sure you have a feel for your stroke—and the greens— so that when you get out on the course, nothing takes you by surprise.

Typically, you have already stretched and hit some balls before arriving at the putting green, so your body is already loose. Start by hitting three or

---

BEST TIP: Abbreviated Warm-Up

The sad truth is that most golfers don't give themselves enough time to warm up properly before a round. If you've only got five minutes to putt before you're called to the first tee, here's what to do. Spend two minutes getting a feel for speed by putting back and forth across the length of the practice green. Each time, try to stop the ball just short of the fringe. Use the remaining time to hit dead-straight three-footers and short breaking putts. Limit yourself to only one ball on the short putts; this intensifies your focus and eases you into an on-course mind-set.

—Mike McGetrick, *GOLF Magazine*
Top 100 Teacher

To bolster confidence, finish your warm-up with a few short ones.

four long putts—30 feet or more—to get a feel for the speed of the greens. Don't worry about making the putts or even getting them close; you're hitting them merely for information. Once you have a sense for how the green is rolling, move in to about 20 feet. Again, don't worry about making anything.

Hit another 3 or 4 putts, and consider them successful if your tempo feels good.

Then hit a couple of 10-foot putts that break, just to see if grain is going to be a big factor. Move in and roll a few from seven feet or so, then finish up with five or six putts from three feet. These short putts let you finish your warm-up with the sound of the ball dropping in the hole ringing in your ears. The key to the warm-up is to cover most of the situations you might see on the course, but with different goals. Keeping pressure to a minimum will keep you loose and confident going into your round.

Practicing at Home

What golfer hasn't hit a few putts into a glass on the living room carpet? It's a time-honored tradition. It is not a good way to work on reading greens or distance control—carpets have a way of actually throwing off your feel for speed—but there are plenty of valuable things you can do at home when weather or a lack of time keeps you away from the course.

The most obvious work you can do is on your setup. In fact, you should make regular check-ins with a full-length mirror. Here's a reminder of what to look for: Facing the mirror, check to see that your feet are 15 to 20 inches apart, the ball is positioned opposite a point just left of your chest's center, and the angle of the putter shaft is vertical, not angled forward or back. Also, make sure that your weight is evenly distributed between both feet. From the down-the-line view, make sure your hands are directly underneath your shoulders and your eyes are over the ball. If you draw imaginary lines across your feet, knees, hips, and shoulders, they should all be parallel to each other.

Home is also a good place to work on stroke mechanics. Find some parallel lines on a rug or tiled floor and you have a perfect guide for a square putterface and a straight-back, straight-through path. Also, try taking your address with your putterface against a doorjamb and making strokes so the face hits the doorjamb at the place in your stance where the ball would be. Making contact with such a big, flat surface provides great sensory feedback and helps train you to get the putterface square at impact.

Want to really challenge yourself? Try the drill Johnny Miller used to hone his control of the putterhead: Lay a dime on a smooth floor and address it as you would a ball. Then make a stroke and try to hit the edge of the dime without banging the putterhead down. Only if you make a perfect stroke will the dime slide across the floor.

Equipment

Ask most Tour pros what the best putter on the market is, and you'd have a hard time getting a straight answer. Endorsement deals aside, if they're putting well, they'll say whatever putter they're using is the best. If they're in a slump, their putter is the worst, a piece of trash. In fact, they've probably already switched to something else. Since hundreds of thousands of dollars rest on a handful of putts on Sunday, it's understandable if they're impatient when their current flatstick isn't cooperating. If their mallet-shaped head isn't sinking putts, maybe they'll go to a blade, or a heel-toe model. Whatever works.

The point is not that you should have a stableful of putters to choose from, but that the only real rule of what makes a putter good is *if it sinks putts*.

That being said, there are some guidelines for picking the best putter for you: It should feel comfortable in your hands; you should like the feel of it as it swings back and through and the sensation you get when it hits the ball; and you should like the way it looks. Looking down at something that pleases your eye engenders confidence, and you can never have too much of that.

Like any other purchase, however, it's smart to know all your options before you make a choice. The following few pages detail the various specifications and styles to consider.

Specs and Options

Shaft Length

The length of the shaft is important because putters are designed to be held at the end of the grip. If the putter is too long and you have to choke up, it changes the balance and feel of the head. So, unless you prefer to crouch over the ball, choose a shaft length that allows you stand fairly erect and extend your arms straight down from your shoulders. Most putters are available in a variety of lengths, but the accepted standard is 35 inches. Experiment to find the length that's best for you.

Lie Angle

This is the angle formed between the shaft and the ground when the putterhead is soled flat. There are a couple of reasons why this is important. First, most putters feature a few degrees of loft, so if the putterhead is not flat on the ground, the face will actually point left or right of your intended target. Therefore, the lie of whatever putter you use should fit your natural stance. Second, it's important to set up with your eyes over the ball for a clear view of the line; if the lie of the putter is too flat (imagine putting with a driver), it will be impossible to sole the putter properly and still position your eyes over the ball.

Many popular putters on the market come in a choice of lies: upright, standard, and flat. Be sure the putter you choose has the appropriate lie, and if it doesn't, see if other lies are available in the same model. A trained PGA pro will help fit you for the proper lie, and most putters can be special ordered with a custom lie if necessary.

Head Style

A look through the history of putters will reveal some pretty bizarre-looking clubs—the putterhead shaped like a hot dog always comes to mind—but for all intents and purposes, there are three basic head shapes to choose from: Heel-toe weighted, mallet, and blade. Heel-toe weighted means the majority of the weight in the head is distributed at the ends—the heel and the toe—with almost no weight behind the sweet spot. The advantage to this style is that if you make contact toward the heel or toe, the head has less of a tendency to twist, and more energy is transmitted to the ball than if the head had an even distribution of weight. Heel-toe weighted putters are generally the most forgiving of mishits, and are therefore the most popular style on the market. The trade-off, however, is that there is less feedback transmitted to the hands on off-center hits, so you won't always know when you've missed the sweet spot. Without a clear reminder that you've goofed, you have to be careful about breeding bad habits.

Mallet putterheads are shaped like a semicircle, with variations among different brands and models. They're generally bigger than the average heel-toe weighted model, which, for some golfers, makes them easier to align and swing on a straight path. Some mallets have the majority of their head weight distributed around the perimeter, which has the same forgiving effect of heel-toe weighting. In that case, the only thing that makes one better than the other is how it putts, feels, and looks to you.

This mallet putter is heel-toe weighted for forgiveness on mishits.

Once popular, the blade putter is now used mostly by golf purists.

Find the Sweet Spot

Most putters have a little line etched into the top of the putterhead to aid in alignment. These lines are almost always exactly halfway between the heel and toe of the putterhead, which, in some cases, is not where you will find the sweet spot! So, here's how you do find the actual sweet spot: Hold the putter by the shaft, between your thumb and forefinger, and let it hang in front of you. Using the end of a tee, tap along the face gently until the putterhead doesn't twist one way or the other. When the tapping makes the head swing straight back and through—like a pendulum—you've found the real sweet spot.

Blade putters were popular in the 1970s and earlier, but they're mostly found in the bags of golf purists these days. Most blades consist of a small, skinny head with the weight evenly distributed from heel to toe. As a result, they're less forgiving: Putts hit toward the ends twist the head and come off the face with reduced energy. The advantage of the blade is that the putterhead's lines are generally clean and uncluttered, which some golfers find easier to align. And there's no mystery: If a putt feels solid and goes straight, you know you've made a good stroke and hit the sweet spot.

Offset Hosel vs. Standard Hosel

Most putters nowadays are offset, which means the neck of the putterhead is bent forward, so the shaft

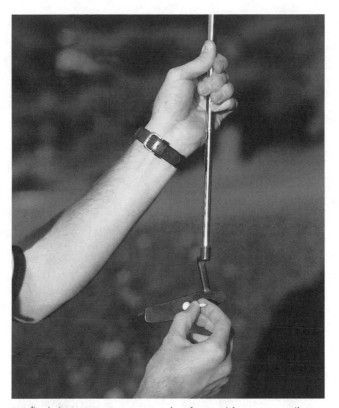

To find the sweet spot, tap the face with a tee until you find the point where the head doesn't twist.

is slightly closer to the target than the face. There is no real mechanical advantage to the offset hosel, but many golfers feel that it gives a better view of the putterface, making it easier to aim. At the same time, it can be argued that standard hosels, with the shaft and putterface in a straight line, make alignment less complicated. In the end, it's a matter of personal taste.

Head Material

You'll find putterheads made from all sorts of different materials: steel, brass, copper, aluminum, even graphite and wood. No material putts better

The offset hosel sets the shaft forward and can aid in face alignment.

than any other, although some—like brass—have a slightly softer feel at impact. Steel is the most common material: it's inexpensive and can be cast into any shape with relative ease.

Face Material

Until recently, the face was always made of the same material as the putterhead. Now many manufacturers are putting plastic or rubber inserts in the faces of steel or beryllium copper putterheads to reduce the shock of impact. The resulting softer feel is only better if that's what you prefer. If you play hard-feeling, two-piece golf balls, these inserts may bring a welcome mellowness to contact, which can feel better in the hands.

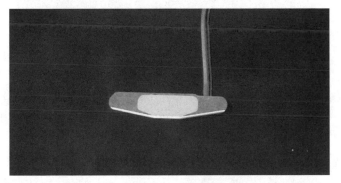

Insert putters are designed to soften the feel of hard balls.

Weight

The general rule of thumb has always been that lighter putters are more effective on fast greens, while heavier putters are more suitable for slower greens. Obviously, it depends on the individual, but as you experiment with different weights, you'll find that heavy putters are great for making long, smooth strokes but more difficult to control on shorter ones. If you're going to own one putter, it makes sense to choose one that feels like it's somewhere in the middle. That way it can be effective no matter what the speed of the greens.

Grip Size

This is largely about personal preference, and most putters don't come with grip-size options. But there is something you should know: The thicker the grip, the easier it is to immobilize the hands and wrists. Thinner grips have a tendency to sit in the fingers and encourage mobility in the hands and wrists. If you feel like this is happening or you simply have large hands, talk to your local pro about switching to a thicker grip or building up the one you use. But be aware that a thicker grip adds weight to the end of the putter, which changes the balance of the club.

Classics and Oddities

Suppose you don't want to be a sheep. You take a look around and decide you don't like any of the putters that are popular in the current market. Suppose you want to be a lone wolf. In that case, you can go in one of two directions: classic or weird.

Most classic putters were first produced in the 1960s or earlier. They earn the "classic" designation because of a certain timelessness: As technology evolves, they remain popular because of a simplicity of design and superior feel. One such putter is the Titleist Bulls Eye, a brass, center-shafted blade that was introduced in the 1930s. It can still be found in pro shops today, and although it isn't as popular as it used to be, a survey of PGA Tour pros would probably reveal that more own a Bulls Eye than don't.

Another classic design is the flange putter, which is like a blade, except there's a small flange on the back of the head. Most of the classic putters of the 1950s, such as the MacGregor IMG and the Wilson 8802, were flanged designs. Today, these putters are bought and sold by collectors for hundreds of

Classic putters are preferred for their simple design and pure feel.

dollars, and there are several models currently on the market that are based on their designs. Flanged putters are usually heel-shafted and, like a blade, require near-perfect contact to produce good results. But one thing you can count on with a classic putter: It looks awfully good sitting in your bag.

Not so with weird putters. There are countless small companies and small-time inventors trying to make a splash in a very crowded putter market. The pressure to create something that will revolutionize putting has inspired some pretty strange-looking offerings, usually with the claim that they will change your game forever. Any such promises should be taken with a healthy grain of salt, but feel free to experiment with "alternative" designs if you wish. You'll find them mostly in mail-order catalogs and discount golf shops, and you never know, you might find your perfect putter.

Occasionally, a weird putter will find its way into the hands of a Tour pro, and even more occasionally, that pro will win a televised tournament using it. That immediately legitimizes the company that made it—at least temporarily. For example, in the 1983 Los Angeles Open, then 52-year-old Gene Littler charged to the third-round lead, one-putting nine greens with something called the Basakwerd putter, which featured a hosel that connected with the toe of the putterhead. During the next two days, the club's manufacturer, a little-known company called Orizaba, sold 7,000 Basakwerds.

In 1986, Jack Nicklaus shot a stunning final-round 65 to win The Masters using the Response ZT putter from MacGregor, a heel-toe model with a giant head, more than twice as big as the average putter on the market. MacGregor took 70,000 orders for the ZT the week following the tournament, but just as quickly, interest in the club died, as many golfers found feel to be lacking in the giant head. The lesson of these stories is actually a good one to keep in mind when you're in the market for any putter, regular or not-so-regular: Don't make a purchase based on how a particular putter works for someone else. Always try it for yourself before you buy.

Who Needs a Putter?

When all is said and done, it's not the putter that makes putts, it's the golfer. And if the golfer is feeling particularly confident, it doesn't matter what kind of putter he's using—or whether he's even using a putter at all.

Consider the story of Ben Crenshaw at the 1987 Ryder Cup matches at Muirfield Village. In a singles match against Europe's Eamonn Darcy, Crenshaw had quickly fallen three down after only six holes when he broke his putter in anger. The Rules of Golf don't allow you to replace a club broken in anger in the middle of a round, so Crenshaw was forced to play the remaining 12 holes without a putter. Widely considered to have one of the best putting strokes ever, Crenshaw started using his 1-iron on the green—and fought back to go one up with two holes remaining. Unfortunately, his brilliant comeback fell short when he lost the last two holes because of some wild shots. It just goes to show you that putting is important, but it's not the only key to scoring. Maybe there is some value in whacking a few drives off rubber mats after all.